Vanishing World

by

PHILIP A. SAUVAIN

Breakaway 6

HULTON EDUCATIONAL PUBLICATIONS

Contents

EARTHQUAKES

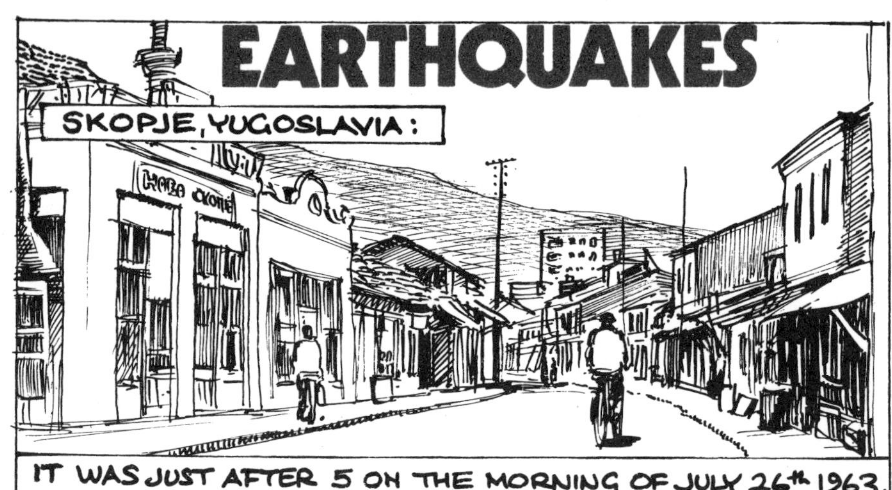

IT WAS JUST AFTER 5 ON THE MORNING OF JULY 26th 1963. ONE OR TWO PEOPLE WERE MAKING THEIR WAY TO WORK WHEN...

IN THE SPACE OF TWO OR THREE SECONDS THE TOWN WAS SHAKEN BY A DEVASTATING EARTHQUAKE.

A TRAIN AT THE RAILWAY STATION WAS DERAILED AND 20 PEOPLE KILLED: THE STATION BUILDINGS CRUMPLED.

THE ARMY CLUB WAS CUT IN TWO LEAVING HALF INTACT AND HALF AS A PILE OF RUBBLE.

THE LARGEST HOTEL IN THE TOWN WAS RUINED.

WATER, TELEPHONE AND ELECTRICITY SERVICES FAILED.

The devastated town could only communicate with other areas by radio. Within hours firemen were fighting the fires in the town and teams of rescue workers were making their way to Skopje, together with lorries carrying supplies. Skopje, a town of 200,000 people, had suffered one of the worst earthquakes of modern times. People ran through the town dazed and shaken by the disaster. Because the earthquake had struck the town so early in the morning many people were half clothed or dressed in pyjamas. Earthquakes give little warning of their arrival. One minute the town was sleeping peacefully, the next minute 100,000 people were homeless. Over 1000 people were killed at Skopje and relief poured into the town from all over the world. Doctors, nurses, even mobile hospitals were rushed to Yugoslavia to help soldiers and civilians clear up the aftermath of the disaster.

Skopje was just one of many earthquakes. In 1923 over 140,000 people were killed in a terrible Japanese earthquake whilst in 1556 nearly one million people were killed in an earthquake disaster in North Western China. There have been earthquakes in the United Kingdom in recent times, although fortunately these have been mild compared with those in the areas of the world most likely to suffer earthquake damage.

THINGS TO DO	
1.	Find out about earthquakes. Is there any way of obtaining advance warning of a major earthquake? How frequent are earthquakes? What is a seismologist? Do you think man will ever be able to control earthquakes?
2.	Which areas of the world are most likely to suffer earthquake damage? Draw a map to show these earthquake zones. What do you notice about the position of these areas on the map?
3.	Find out about earth tremors in Britain. When was the last British earthquake?
4.	Look at the photograph showing the aftermath of the Skopje earthquake disaster. How would you raise money for a disaster fund to help the victims of such a catastrophe? What do you think would be the best way of bringing home to people in this country what the hardship and suffering caused by an earthquake can mean? Find out more about the relief organisations in Britain and the methods they use in order to get support for their campaigns.

VOLCANOES

TRISTAN DA CUNHA IS ONE OF THE LONELIEST ISLANDS IN THE WORLD SITUATED IN THE SOUTH ATLANTIC HALF-WAY BETWEEN SOUTH AMERICA AND SOUTH AFRICA.

TRISTAN DA CUNHA

ON THE 9th OCTOBER 1961 RUMBLINGS WERE HEARD ON THE ISLAND AND THE WALLS OF SOME OF THE HOUSES STARTED TO CRACK.

A SMALL VOLCANO HAD ERUPTED CLOSE TO THE VILLAGE OF EDINBURGH WHERE MOST OF THE PEOPLE LIVED.

ON THE FOLLOWING DAY THE 305 INHABITANTS OF THE ISLAND LEFT TRISTAN DA CUNHA LEAVING BEHIND COWS, SHEEP AND MANY PERSONAL POSSESSIONS.

REYKJAVIK
WESTMANN ISLANDS

THE WESTMANN ISLANDS ARE JUST OVER 100 KILOMETRES FROM REYKJAVIK, THE CAPITAL OF ICELAND.

ABOUT TEN YEARS AFTER THE TRISTAN DA CUNHA ERUPTION THE PEOPLE OF THE WESTMANN ISLANDS SUFFERED A SIMILAR CALAMITY.

RUMBLINGS HERALDED A SPECTACULAR VOLCANIC ERUPTION

WITHIN A MATTER OF HOURS THE ISLAND'S HARBOUR WAS THREATENED BY THE LAVA FLOW.
THE TEMPERATURE OF THE SEA ROSE...

The scientists who study volcanoes are hopeful that in time they will be able to forecast with accuracy just when a volcano will erupt. But there is little hope that in the foreseeable future they will be able to prevent them from erupting.

Over 300 houses on the island of Heimaey were buried by rock and ash. A prosperous fishing town had been hit by a catastrophic volcanic eruption.

Tristan da Cunha and the Westmann Islands can be matched by many other areas of the world subject to volcanic action. On Mount Etna in Sicily thousands live on the mountain slopes and risk the likelihood of volcanic eruption because the soil from the volcanic ash is so good. Periodically the land they have won for vineyards is threatened by lava flows and volcanic ash.

The volcanic areas of the world are in one sense part of the vanishing world since farmland, as at Tristan da Cunha or Mount Etna, can be destroyed and people's livelihoods (as at the fishing port of Heimaey) can be threatened. But volcanoes also produce new land. For instance, a new island erupted off the Azores in 1958. It was called Ilha Nova meaning the "new island".

THINGS TO DO

1. How is volcanic activity made to work for the benefit of man? Find out about the schemes which have been developed in Iceland, Italy and New Zealand.

2. Volcanic ash can be extremely fertile. What do you think of people who deliberately farm the slopes of a volcano knowing full well that sooner or later the volcano will erupt?

3. Trace a large outline map of the world and on that map locate with dots all the major active volcanoes. What do you notice about the pattern of dots you have produced? Compare your map with the map you have already drawn of the earthquake zones (question 2, page 5).

4. The photograph shows the volcano Vesuvius in Italy. How would you recognise a volcano on the ground? What do they always seem to have in common?

5. Find out something about the former volcanoes of the British Isles. What is left today to remind us that our land once suffered from volcanic activity?

FLOODING

Diana Lewis and Sally Bush were friends living close to each other and attending the same school.

On the March night when the floods came they stayed late at school playing badminton.

The river looked full though they couldn't see clearly in the gloom from the top of the brightly-lit bus.

But when they looked outside the river was already in flood.

"Quick! Upstairs!" said Sally.

"What about Mrs. Tibbett next door?" asked her mother. "She's had to sleep downstairs since she hurt her hip."

"We'll go," said Sally. "Come on Diana. You collect anything valuable, Mum, and go upstairs. We'll take Mrs. Tibbett up to her bedroom." Diana decided to stay with Mrs Tibbett for the floodwater made it foolish for her to try to make her way home and she and Sally agreed that Mrs. Tibbett needed someone by her, just in case.

The floodwater rose higher and Sally was worried when it started to seep through the front door. By now the street was like a river. Later that night rescue workers came by in a boat.

"Everyone O.K.?" they shouted. Fortunately the flood was going down rapidly and by next morning things were nearly back to normal. But mud covered the street and in the houses lower down the carpets were ruined.

"What excitement!" said Diana when her father called for her. "Everything all right at home?"

"Aye," he said. "Good job you phoned us from Mrs Tibbett's. They say someone was drowned in Victoria Lane."

THINGS TO DO

1. Is flooding a serious problem in Britain? Find out when flooding last occurred in your district. See if you can discover what damage was done. If you can manage to find the actual dates of the floods then you could make a trip to the library or the newspaper offices in order to look at the local newspaper files. You should be able to find the past issues of the paper describing these floods. Further investigation may help you to find other newspaper descriptions of bad floods in your area in the last hundred years or so.

2. The photograph shows flooding in Kenya. Is flooding a serious problem in the world? When and where were the most recent severe floods in the world?

3. Whenever a river floods some homes are usually inundated, such as those described in the picture sequence opposite. Why do you think people live in houses close to rivers which are known to flood? Do you have any sympathy for them when they are caught out?

HURRICANES & STORMS

TOM DERWENT WAS SURE HE WAS RIGHT WHEN THE DISCUSSION IN CLASS GOT ROUND TO THE SUBJECT OF A RECENT HURRICANE IN THE CARIBBEAN

BERNARD WALSH CONTRADICTED HIM:

"FROM WHAT HE'S TOLD ME IT MUST HAVE BEEN TERRIBLE. THOUSANDS OF HOUSES WERE DAMAGED AND ELEVEN PEOPLE WERE KILLED.

SOME HOUSES HAD THEIR END WALLS RIPPED OFF BY THE GALE.

ONE OF THE FLOODLIGHTS CAME DOWN AT THE SHEFFIELD UNITED GROUND AT BRAMALL LANE."

PAULINE CRANE JOINED IN:

Mr. Slater, the geography teacher, asked her how she knew.

"My Gran lives near there and she told me. She said it was caused by a gale called Pauline." The class laughed.

"That's why I know. She always teases me about it when I go there."

"It really is amazing what the wind can do," said Mr. Slater. "Some of the hurricanes in the Caribbean can cause terrible damage. Some winds get up to 200 k.p.h. (about 125 m.p.h.). Timber houses just disintegrate into matchwood, roofs are blown off and boats can be wrecked."

"Why do they give them girls' names?" asked Pauline.

"I don't know," said Mr. Slater. "You'd better see if you can find out. It's a bit unfair on women, I must admit."

"Has there ever been any really serious disaster in this country caused by wind?" asked Susan Blake.

"Well there are always accidents at sea," said Mr. Slater. "Apart from that I suppose the worst was the Tay Bridge disaster of 1879. It was just after Christmas when the central portion of the bridge was blown down during a tremendous gale. Unfortunately a train was crossing at the time and 73 people were drowned."

THINGS TO DO

1. The picture on this page was drawn for the magazine the *Illustrated London News* for an issue published in 1880 immediately after the disaster to the Tay Bridge. Describe the bridge and the attempted rescue scene depicted here. See if you can find out the reasons why the bridge blew down.

2. Find out about hurricanes, cyclones and typhoons and their effect on areas like the Caribbean where they are relatively common. What causes them? What effects can they have? Is there anything man can do to reduce their effects or to prevent their occurrence in the first place? What are the differences between hurricanes, tornadoes, whirlwinds, cyclones and typhoons?

3. Does the wind have any effect at all on the surface of the rocks of the earth? Find out what happens in desert lands.

4. What effect can gales have on tall buildings and tall vehicles? Find out about the ways in which designers take the likelihood of high winds into consideration when designing vehicles and buildings.

LAND~SLIDES

THERE ARE FEW AREAS OF THE WORLD WHICH HAVE NOT BEEN THREATENED BY AVALANCHES AND LANDSLIDES AT SOME TIME OR OTHER. THE WORST DISASTER OF THIS TYPE IN BRITAIN OCCURRED ON 21st OCTOBER 1966 AT ABERFAN IN SOUTH WALES

ABERFAN IS A COALMINING VILLAGE, ONCE DOMINATED BY A GIANT SLAG HEAP. IN 1966 HEAVY RAIN DRENCHED THE AREA AND LOOSENED THE MATERIAL IN THE TIP

A MOVING MASS OF SLUDGE AND MINE DEBRIS SLIPPED DOWN AND BURIED SEVERAL HOUSES AND THE VILLAGE SCHOOL, KILLING 116 CHILDREN.

AT RANRAHICA IN PERU MANY HUNDREDS OF PEOPLE HAD LOST THEIR LIVES FOUR YEARS EARLIER IN JANUARY 1962 AS THE RESULT OF A NATURAL LANDSLIDE

THE TROUBLE STARTED HIGH ABOVE THE VILLAGE ON THE SLOPES OF Mt. HUASCARAN WHERE SNOW WAS MELTING.

A HUGE RIVER OF ICE PICKED UP MUD AND ROCKS AND RUSHED DOWN THE SLOPES

IT DESTROYED MANY FARMS AND COVERED THE VILLAGE OF RANRAHICA WHICH LAY AT THE FOOT OF THE MOUNTAIN.

THE MUD AND ICE LAY EIGHT METRES THICK ON THE GROUND AND IN LESS THAN TEN MINUTES THE VILLAGE DISAPPEARED FROM THE SURFACE OF THE EARTH.

FURTHER READING

Avalanches and landslides are natural processes. Because of them mountain slopes and valley sides are shaped and eroded by the weather. This process is known as *weathering*. In a way this really is the "vanishing world", for if these processes of erosion and weathering are allowed to go unchecked the world's mountains will gradually be eroded over a period of millions of years and will end up as silt and mud carried away by rivers and streams and dumped in the sea.

At the same time waves at the coast undermine cliffs and cause rockfalls and landslides. Over a period of time the sea will gradually inundate the land as it has many times in the past.

Man can protect the land against the sea, however, by building sea walls as a defence, but it is not easy to protect mountains and hills against avalanches and landslides. Every year there are accidents with groups of people being engulfed by avalanches.

Perhaps the one type of landslide which is unforgivable is that caused by the collapse of a man-made mountain, such as at Aberfan in 1966 where a school was engulfed, or at the Belgian mining village of Moulins-sous-Fleron in 1961 when several people were killed by the collapse of a slag heap.

THINGS TO DO

1. Find out about avalanches and landslides. What are the main causes of these land movements? Is this a serious problem in Britain? Is it possible to control movements of this type?

2. Avalanches and landslides are natural movements of the earth and over millions of years have helped to shape the earth's surface. If this is the case is it right for man to attempt to interfere with the process?

3. The photograph shows a scene after the terrible disaster at Aberfan in 1966. In a sense this accident happened because we needed coal. Otherwise there would have been no slag heap. Coal mining is a notoriously dangerous occupation and the hazards of living in a coal mining area also include damage from subsidence as the land surface gives way above mine workings deep underground. Has the price for coal in terms of human lives, pollution and destruction of lovely countryside been worth it? Discuss this topic with your friends.

SOIL EROSION

OVER A PERIOD OF HUNDREDS OF YEARS FARMERS IN MANY PARTS OF THE WORLD HAVE CLEARED TREES, PUT THEIR CATTLE AND SHEEP TO GRAZE ON NATURAL GRASSLAND AND PLOUGHED UP LARGE FIELDS TO GROW CROPS SUCH AS WHEAT AND BARLEY.

DURING HOT DRY SUMMERS THE SOIL HAS OFTEN BAKED HARD AND CRACKED AND CRUMBLED.

IN HIGH WINDS FINE SOIL HAS BEEN BLOWN AWAY WHERE PREVIOUSLY TREES OR GRASSLAND KEPT THE SOIL MOIST AND HELD IT TOGETHER.

AT TIMES OF TORRENTIAL RAIN, GULLIES HAVE BEEN FORMED ON HILL SLOPES....

...AND MUCH OF THE SOIL HAS BEEN WASHED AWAY AS MUD.

FARMERS AND SCIENTISTS HAVE PUT THEIR HEADS TOGETHER, WORRIED BY THIS PROBLEM OF SOIL EROSION.

IF NOTHING IS DONE ABOUT IT THE LAND WILL DISAPPEAR AND SOIL WHICH TOOK THOUSANDS OF YEARS TO FORM WILL VANISH COMPLETELY.

ONE SOLUTION IS TO PLANT TREES AS WINDBREAKS.

ANOTHER IS TO PLOUGH ROUND A HILL RATHER THAN UP AND DOWN IT.

This is known as contour ploughing. It works because it prevents gullies forming in the furrows. In the past, heavy rain collected in the furrows and washed soil downhill. After a hill has been contour-ploughed the water simply stays in the furrows almost as if the hill had been surrounded by a number of parallel circular canals. Sometimes farmers plough small areas of their fields only. The rest of the land is then devoted to grassland or other crops. In this way they prevent much of the soil blowing away in a high wind.

Irrigation has also helped, for this has meant that the soil is less likely to become bone-dry. Water gives the soil moisture which binds it together. In many parts of the world complex schemes have been developed involving close control of rivers and their tributary streams. At times of heavy rainfall dams can hold back flood-water. In this way engineers hope to protect the land against sudden floods and at the same time provide a relia-ble and permanent source of water for irrigation purposes.

An expert sums up the problem of soil erosion.

"Heavy rainstorms can wash away in an hour soil which has taken hundreds of years to accumulate."

THINGS TO DO

1. Is soil erosion a serious problem in the British Isles? Find out more about the soils of your home area.

2. Imagine you are a farmer in one of the areas shown in the photographs on this page. What would your reaction be if a Government expert told you to alter your farming methods in order to prevent soil erosion? How would you tackle the task of getting over to farmers the serious nature of the soil erosion problem?

3. Does soil erosion occur natur-ally or is it always brought about by the misuse of the land by man? Find out more about the problem of soil erosion in the world.

4. Try to find examples of ways in which the actions of man have accelerated the process of soil erosion. What happened to the prairie lands of North America? See if you can find out how grazing animals such as sheep and goats have contributed to the soil erosion problem in some parts of the world.

FOREST FIRE

MILLIONS OF POUNDS'
WORTH OF DAMAGE IS
CAUSED EVERY YEAR BY
FIRES IN THE WORLD'S
FORESTS. FIRE-FIGHTING IS
A MAJOR OCCUPATION FOR
FORESTRY OFFICIALS.

A FIRE STARTED IN A
CANADIAN FOREST :
THERE'S A
FIRE AT
GRID 38 !
THE NEWS WAS RELAYED TO H.Q.
AND PLOTTED ON A MAP.

WITHIN MINUTES THE FIRE PREVENTION
OFFICER HAD PLANNED THE ACTION HE
WAS GOING TO TAKE ...

A PLANE TOOK OFF FOR A VISUAL INSPECTION
OF THE SITE OF THE FIRE.

MEANWHILE A SPECIAL PLANE WAS BEING LOADED WITH
WATER AT AN AIRSTRIP NEARBY.

O.K. —
LET'S GO !

AS THE WATER BOMBER FLEW LOW OVER THE FOREST FIRE THE BOMB DOORS OPENED
TO RELEASE A GREAT WAVE OF WATER SPECIALLY MIXED WITH CHEMICALS.

The plane made several successful runs, each time reloading with water by skimming low over the surface of a lake. This fire was put out with the minimum of fuss, but behind the successful mission there was much careful planning.

Fighting a fire with water dropped from the air is rather like conducting a military operation. In fact the whole business of fighting forest fires at ground level or from the air is one that requires careful planning and meticulous organisation. The difficulties faced by foresters are partly due to the weather, for in hot dry summers the forests get so dry that the slightest spark can set them ablaze. Even lightning can start a fire, but often it is just carelessness on the part of a visitor to the forest. Forest look-out towers are manned constantly in dry weather but despite the vigilance of the foresters fires can get quickly out of hand. Severe bush fires regularly cause damage in Australia or California. In 1961 a brush fire set part of Hollywood alight and the luxury homes of many famous filmstars were destroyed in the blaze. In Australia bush fires have frequently threatened the livelihood of farmers during the hot dry season.

THINGS TO DO

1. The photograph was taken in a Welsh forest. Find out more about the dangers from fire in the forests of Britain. Is it as serious a problem as in Australia, California or Canada?

2. Compare the problems of the forestry official with those of the city firemen (see page 18). What are the similarities? What are the differences?

3. How are forests planned in order to try to keep the danger from fire down to the minimum?

4. What has happened to the natural forests of Britain? Two thousand years ago there were great areas of forest land and hundreds of years ago there were still forests such as Sherwood near Nottingham. These were mainly deciduous forests (trees shedding their leaves in the autumn). Are forest fires a problem in deciduous woodland areas? Are they a problem in tropical forests at the Equator?

FIRE ALARM
WHEN THE ALARM WENT AT 10.40 PM THE MEN OF THE FIRE BRIGADE HAD LITTLE IDEA THAT THIS WOULD BE ONE OF THE BIGGEST IN THE TOWN FOR MANY YEARS.

A LARGE HOTEL WAS ON FIRE AND THE FLAMES WERE THREATENING NEARBY BUILDINGS. THE WIND GOT UP ...

...AND THE WORST HAPPENED. TWO OTHER BUILDINGS CAUGHT FIRE.

55 FIRE APPLIANCES AND NEARLY 200 FIREMEN FOUGHT THE BLAZE.

AFTER 18 HOURS THEY GOT IT UNDER CONTROL. £3 MILLION WORTH OF DAMAGE HAD BEEN DONE.

AMBULANCE
AMBULANCE
THREE FIREMEN WERE TAKEN TO HOSPITAL ...

AND TWELVE CARS PARKED IN THE HOTEL CAR PARK WERE COMPLETELY BURNT OUT.

Fortunately there was no loss of life. Other fires have caused terrible losses, especially where they have involved hotels or department stores with many storeys. The worst ever fire in one building caused the deaths of nearly 1,700 people at a theatre in China in 1845. Ironically fire was probably first discovered in China over 500,000 years ago. It is one of man's major discoveries and yet when uncontrolled is a principal hazard to life in any built-up area. Every major city in the world must take adequate precautions against outbreaks of fire which could lead, if unchecked, to the complete destruction of large areas – something which happened during the Great Fire of London in 1666.

Unfortunately new developments in technology have added extra hazards to the life of the fireman. Tower blocks of flats and offices can trap people who have the misfortune to be caught in the upper storeys. Most major cities alert helicopters for rescue in such situations. Asphyxiation is another major problem these days owing to the use in buildings of materials and furnishings made from plastics and other new materials. Recent fires, such as that in the Summerland Pleasure Centre on the Isle of Man or the fire which swept through a French dance-hall, show the terrible effects which can occur when some new materials are set alight.

THINGS TO DO

1. Find out more about the problems of fighting fires in cities. How has modern technology assisted the fireman? What developments have made his job more difficult?

2. Could a catastrophic fire such as the Great Fire of London occur again in one of the great cities of the world? What combination of circumstances might lead to disaster?

3. How is the fire service organised in your district? How long does it take on average for the fire brigade to get to the scene of a fire?

4. What precautions should the householder take to minimise the risk of fire? What precautions does a hotel owner have to take? What special precautions are necessary in a tower block of flats?

5. What action should you take on discovering an outbreak of fire at home? Prepare a list of Action Points.

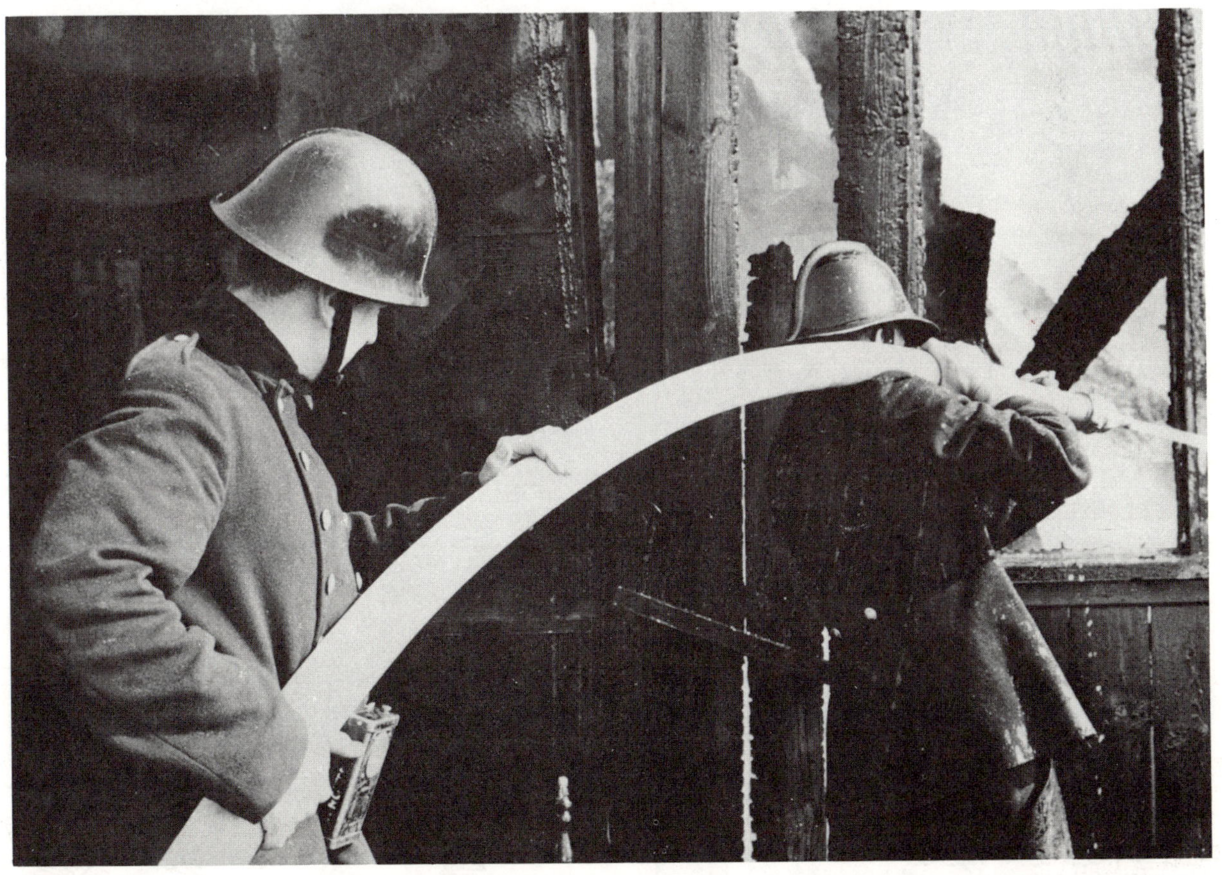

VANDALISM

'IT HAS BEEN A BAD WEEK FOR VANDALISM' SAID THE TV NEWSREADER ON THE LOCAL 6.0 PM NEWS PROGRAMME — AND MOST OF THE VIEWERS AGREED
A SLOGAN HAD BEEN PAINTED ON THE WALL OF A LOCAL CHURCH
FEED THE POOR OF ASIA
...ABSOLUTELY DISGUSTING.
FOOTBALL SUPPORTERS - RETURNING WITH THEIR LOSING TEAM - HAD BROKEN UP A RAILWAY CARRIAGE.
NO MORE FOOTBALL TRAINS FROM THIS STATION, THAT'S FOR SURE. WE JUST CAN'T AFFORD IT.
TWO TEN-YEAR-OLD GIRLS PICKED FLOWERS IN THE TOWN'S PARK...
WHILE A GROUP OF APPRENTICES KICKED A FOOTBALL IN THE STREET AND BROKE A SHOP WINDOW AND DENTED TWO CARS.
MR. MARK WARD WAS NOT AMUSED
LOUTS! THAT'S WHAT THEY ARE.

"Oh come now dear," said his wife. "I seem to remember your telling me that when you were at College you once staged a rugby match in the crowded shopping streets of the town."

"That was different," said Mr. Ward. "We knew how to behave. These young hooligans of today don't know any better."

"If that's the case," said his wife, "then surely you had no excuse whatever, whilst the young hooligans as you call them can at least be excused on the grounds that they are incapable of telling right from wrong."

"Very clever!" snarled Mr. Ward.

"At any rate I am sure you could find many cases of vandalism in the past just as bad as those which the press and television make such a fuss of today," said Mrs Ward.

"That's not the point," was the reply. "In the past vandalism was rare – today it is common." The local magistrates sided with Mr. Ward and always came down heavily on cases of vandalism.

"The trouble with the law is that the penalties we can impose are too soft. We really need to be able to give you young vandals something to think about," said a magistrate in court.

THINGS TO DO

1. Mr. Ward justified his acts of hooliganism when at College on the grounds that "we knew how to behave". Do you think this is a sensible way of looking at "pranks" by students or is it even more deplorable that people who claim to know "how to behave" should act like hooligans? Or has the attitude of people to students so changed that even the simplest expression of high spirits is condemned nowadays? Discuss this topic with your friends.

2. Of all the so-called acts of vandalism described on the opposite page would you say that some were worse than others?

3. Is it true to say that these days there is more vandalism? See if you can find out by asking your older friends and relatives.

4. When does a simple act such as picking flowers in a park become an act of vandalism? Is there any difference between two small girls picking the flowers and two teenagers doing the same thing?

Action Litter

Eric Neville and Chris Fielding decided to do something about the litter problem in the small town they lived in. Litter piled up whenever visitors came to town.

Their unauthorised campaign certainly had its effect. Tourists watched the progress of the 'litter wardens' with interest and some resentment.

The regular car park attendants were amused.

Another successful stunt was their sponsored clean-up campaign of the local stream. A team of volunteers cleared several tons of scrap and earned over £100 for charity.

When the local authority started to erect unsightly concrete litter bins, Eric and Chris got up a campaign to have them replaced by more attractive bins.

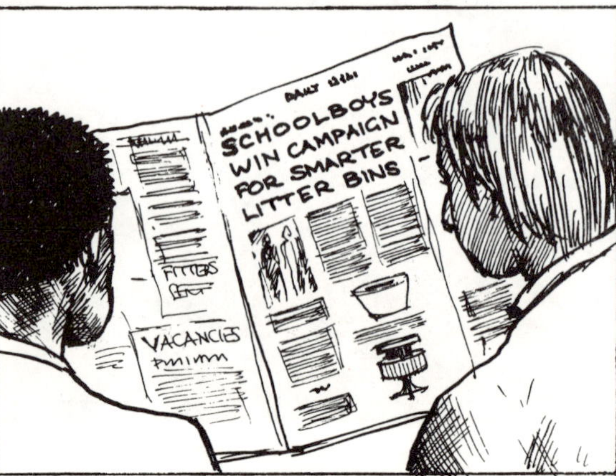

"What next?" asked Eric's sister Sheila. "Getting your names in the paper has made you famous, what with new litter bins and sponsored litter collections. So what's new?"

Eric laughed. "I don't know. Perhaps we'll just take it easy for a while." But things didn't work out quite like that. Chris was reading a magazine at the dentist's when he came across an article showing photographs of various items of foreign litter which had drifted across the Channel.

"There were milk cartons from Germany and France, plastic containers from Denmark and Holland and even a tin from Norway," he told Eric.

"Let's do a coastal survey," said Eric, "but on a big scale. We could get a number of volunteers to help. It would be like clearing the river but designed to show just how badly people misuse the coast." Eric and Chris made plans and with eight of their friends went to the coast one Saturday. They were amazed at the things they collected, but more annoyed by the tar they found on the stones.

"Every other stone has got tar on it," Eric announced. The other members of the team made a systematic count and came to the same conclusion.

"Over 53% of these stones have tar on them somewhere," said Chris. "It's disgusting."

THINGS TO DO

1. Where does the tar on the pebbles come from? Is this a problem at the seaside resorts you have been to on holiday?

2. The photograph on the right shows part of the countryside in Cheshire. How would you combat the problem of litter in areas of great natural beauty? If lots of litter bins are erected and warning notices put up they can look as unsightly as the litter they are supposed to prevent. What is the solution?

3. Do you agree that manufacturers tend to provide too much packaging? Do you think people would return tin cans or cardboard boxes if there was a deposit of 2p on each one?

4. What do you think of the idea of Litter Wardens at the seaside? Would you say it is probably necessary nowadays or would you describe it as "red tape"?

POLLUTING A RIVER

OWEN BURKE (15) AND ANDREW MARSDEN (16) HAD BEEN CONDUCTING A SURVEY INTO THE WAYS IN WHICH THEIR LOCAL RIVER HAD BEEN POLLUTED.
THEY PRESENTED THEIR REPORT TO THE REST OF THE CLASS.

SOME OF THE FACTORIES ON THE BANKS OF THE RIVER ARE NEARLY AS BAD. SOMEONE WE SPOKE TO RECKONED THAT IF YOU FELL IN YOU WOULD HAVE TO BE RUSHED TO HOSPITAL IMMEDIATELY.

"Why bother about fish?" asked one of the girls in the class. "Surely electricity is more important than fish?"

"Possibly," said Andrew," but we all have a duty to ensure that the rivers are as clean as they can be. If there are healthy fish in the river this means a clean river for other activities as well, such as swimming. Why should we put up with open sewers in the twentieth century? We got rid of those a long time ago for normal sewage disposal so why not go the whole way and allow the rivers to become clean and fresh once again?"

"Yes," added Owen. "Don't forget the country needs more water so why not let the rivers supply it? They could do so easily enough, provided people acted now to ensure that river pollution was forbidden by law."

"Which is the worst river in Britain?" asked Judith Browne.

"They say it's the Trent," answered Owen, "but it really depends on the size of river you have in mind. There are probably smaller streams which are even worse. In any case the rivers Mersey, Tyne and Clyde are close runners-up to the Trent in the pollution race. But even these don't hold a candle to the German Rhine, said to be the worst river in Europe."

THINGS TO DO

1. The cartoon drawing from *Punch* (below) shows what a cartoonist thought of the state of the river Thames over a hundred years ago. What do you think was the purpose of this cartoon? What sort of cartoon would you produce today to draw attention to the problem of Britain's polluted rivers?

2. What benefit would *you* get from clean rivers?

3. The photograph shows the salmon ladder at the side of the hydro-electric dam at Pitlochry in Scotland. This allows salmon to swim upstream through a series of artificial pools. Do you think the cost of maintaining freshwater life in our rivers and lakes is worthwhile or is it a waste of money? Why bother about fish?

4. Make a survey of your local rivers on lines similar to that of the survey carried out by Owen Burke and Andrew Marsden.

SMOKE

I'LL NEVER FORGET IT, SUSIE. THAT REALLY WAS A FOG!
I WAS WORKING IN THE CITY OF LONDON AT THAT TIME — NOT FAR FROM THE BANK OF ENGLAND.

YOU COULD HARDLY SEE ACROSS THE STREETS. IT WAS TERRIBLE.

I WORE A HANDKER-CHIEF AS A MASK...

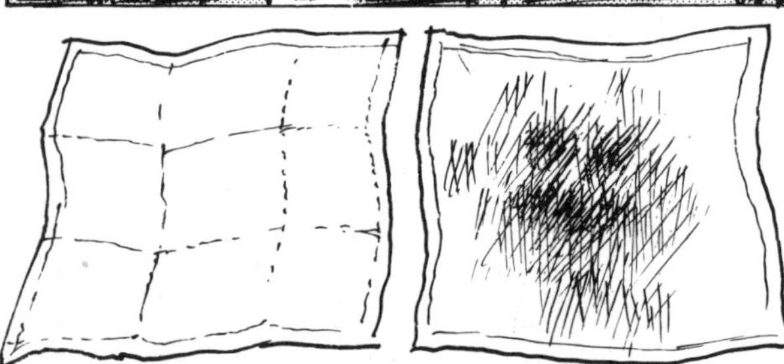
... AND WHEN I GOT HOME I COMPARED IT WITH A CLEAN HANDKERCHIEF. IT WAS FILTHY.

WAS IT REALLY AS BAD AS ALL THAT, DAD?
WELL, ABOUT 700 PEOPLE DIED AS A RESULT OF THAT SMOG AND 10 YEARS EARLIER IN 1952, 4000 PEOPLE DIED IN THE SMOG.

WHAT IS SMOG?
A PRETTY LETHAL MIXTURE OF SMOKE AND FOG SUSIE ...

SINCE 1952 THE GOVERNMENT HAS BROUGHT IN A CLEAN AIR ACT AND THIS WAS ONE REASON WHY FAR FEWER PEOPLE DIED IN THE 1962 SMOG COMPARED WITH THE 1952 SMOG.
BRYTEFYRE SMOKELESS FUELS
WE BREATHE PURER AIR NOW, SUSIE.

Joe Foster was correct in saying that the air in London has become purer but by any standards it is still polluted compared with that of the hills of Wales or Scotland. Smoke from coal is only one form of air pollution. Probably the most important source of air pollution today is the motor car. Los Angeles, a city built for the motor car, suffers from terrible smogs even though the climate of southern California is generally hot and dry and quite unlike the damp and naturally foggy British Isles. The problem is that car exhausts give off carbon monoxide and lead and both of these substances are poisonous. Sulphur dioxide is another major air pollutant given off when fuel is burnt. In one survey it was shown that London had nearly ten times as much sulphur dioxide in the air as a seaside resort and Glasgow was four times as smoky as Cardiff.

After a survey carried out by schoolchildren a Sunday newspaper was able to show that much of the air in Britain was polluted – even in the agricultural areas of eastern England. The method used to measure polluted air was based on a study of lichens – types of fungus found growing on trees, walls and rocks.

the underdeveloped countries of the world today with regard to industrial development? On the one hand the lessons of London, Tokyo and Los Angeles point to restrictions on industrial growth and on the development of the motor vehicle. On the other hand all countries naturally want higher living standards and there is no doubting the fact that effective control of atmospheric pollution costs money. What is your advice?

2. Is air pollution a problem in your district?

THINGS TO DO

1. The *Punch* cartoon on this page was drawn over a hundred years ago and shows a scene during one of the great fogs of Victorian London. The other picture shows an aerial view of the modern Japanese city of Tokyo. Japan is rightly proud of her phenomenal industrial growth but this has sometimes been at the expense of clean air. Pollution of the atmosphere is a major problem in Tokyo. As you have seen, Los Angeles suffers from terrible smogs. How would you advise one of

Pesticides & Chemicals

George Griffiths, a farmworker, left for work at 7.35 am

Five minutes later he passed a tanker at the side of the road – it seemed to be on fire.

50 metres further up the road the tanker driver flagged him down …

George turned his bike round and as luck would have it, saw a patrol car within minutes as he sped towards the phone booth.

The fire brigade was called and an urgent phone call put through to the chemical works asking for expert advice.

The policemen quickly set up road blocks and diverted traffic.

Twenty minutes later a helicopter from the chemical works was on its way to the scene of the accident.

By this time the members of the Fire Brigade had put on breathing apparatus, for the smoke billowing from the lorry made the eyes sting.

"Better safe than sorry!" said the Fire Officer in charge of the operation. When the experts from the chemical works arrived they made a quick inspection and then advised the immediate evacuation of the area. Their advice was sound, for suddenly there was an explosion and a very shaken tanker driver saw his vehicle disintegrate.

George Griffiths had stayed behind to see what would happen and consequently arrived late at work. The farm manager was annoyed at first but calmed down on hearing about the explosion.

"It's time they did something about dangerous liquids in tankers on the roads. One of these days there'll be a really serious accident." George agreed and started up his tractor. His job for the day was applying a pesticide to one of the fields. As he loaded the distributor he wondered whether the chemical used as the crop spray was dangerous in any way.

"Not really," said the farm manager. "It depends how it is used or misused."

"But what about birds?" asked George. "Is it poisonous to creatures other than insects?"

1. Find out about crop spraying. What are the arguments for and against? Was the farm manager right when he dismissed the idea of danger as just depending on how it is used or misused? If there are disadvantages (such as the death of birds) do these outweigh the advantages (such as increased crop yields)? Once again this is a case of examining the cost of looking after the world's wildlife. What are your views?

2. What do you think about the problem of tankers carrying chemicals? Chemical works like the one shown in the photograph below are essential to modern society. Without them there would be no plastics, fewer fabrics and few drugs. But in order to produce goods using raw chemicals some form of transportation is needed and the railways are not necessarily the answer. Yet the chemicals include dangerous acids, poisons and highly explosive or inflammable substances. The dangers of an accident are very real. How would you tackle this problem?

NOISE

MARY BRADLEY AND SARAH JONES WERE INVESTIGATING NOISE AS PART OF A SURVEY INTO POLLUTION WHICH WAS BEING CARRIED OUT BY THEIR SCHOOL.
MARY & SARAH MADE A SURVEY OF THE TOWN FIRST BUT FOUND IT DIFFICULT TO SAY HOW LOUD THE NOISES WERE.
MR. PICKERING THE SCIENCE TEACHER HELPED.
THIS IS WHAT YOU NEED, SARAH.
IT'S A SOUND LEVEL METER. WHEN YOU SWITCH IT ON, A NEEDLE TELLS YOU THE SOUND LEVEL.
dB(A)
SOUND LEVEL METER
NOISE IS MEASURED IN DECIBELS BUT THE SCALE USED IS NOT THE SAME AS A WEIGHT SCALE, FOR INSTANCE
...BUT A READING OF 110 DECIBELS (SAY A JET AIRLINER TAKING OFF) IS 10 TIMES LOUDER THAN A READING OF 100 DECIBELS (SAY THE SOUND OF A MACHINE IN A FACTORY)
IF YOU WEIGH SOMETHING AT 100 kg YOU KNOW IT IS TWICE AS HEAVY AS SOMETHING WEIGHING 50 kg.
110 dBA
100 dBA
90 dBA
SIMILARLY 90 DECIBELS (A HEAVY LORRY 6 METRES AWAY) IS 10 TIMES LOUDER THAN 80 DECIBELS (THE BACK SEAT OF MY OLD CAR)
80 dBA
ACL
AMALGAMATED CONTAINERS LTD
TIR
SCAMMELL

"But what about quiet sounds?" asked Mary. "I suppose they go down to less than 10 decibels."

"Well yes," said Mr. Pickering, "but you wouldn't be able to hear anything. Imagine yourself far out in the hills with only the distant sheep to disturb the quiet. You would still get a reading of about 25 decibels."

"But why are people so concerned about noise?" asked Sarah.

"Well obviously anyone exposed to very loud sounds could go deaf. In fact sound can kill. A noise level of about 140 decibels would cause instant ear damage. Some experts believe that people who spend their working lives with loud noises do in fact suffer eventual deterioration of their hearing."

"Can anything be done about unwanted noises?" asked Mary.

"Yes," said Mr. Pickering. "The Noise Abatement Act gives householders the right to complain about noises to the local Public Health Department. This Department has to investigate the complaint and if they agree that there is a noise which is a nuisance they can order the offenders to "abate" their noise. If this has no effect then your noisy neighbours can be prosecuted!"

"But that's wrong surely?" said Sarah. "It's a free country isn't it?"

3. Do you know any people who work to a perpetual background of noise, as in some textile mills or in a steel works? What do they think about the problem of noise?

4. Look at the two photographs. Find out what the probable reading of a sound level meter would have been had it been placed next to the camera on each of these occasions.

5. Some experts have said that listening to loud music amplified through speakers can lead to early deafness and certainly poorer hearing. What do you think? Is this an old wives' tale?

THINGS TO DO

1. How would you reply to Sarah's last question? What would your reaction be if told to "abate" a noise?

2. Do you regard noise as a serious problem? Is your town noisy? Make a noise survey of an area of your town. See if noise abatement notices should be served to anyone in the district you survey.

RADIOACTIVITY

THE ATOMIC BOMBS DROPPED ON THE JAPANESE CITIES OF HIROSHIMA AND NAGASAKI IN 1945 KILLED MANY PEOPLE YEARS AFTER THE EXPLOSIONS. THEY DIED FROM THE EFFECTS OF RADIOACTIVE FALLOUT

IN THE 1950'S AND 1960'S NUCLEAR TESTS WERE CARRIED OUT BY A NUMBER OF COUNTRIES INCLUDING THE U.K.

MANY PEOPLE PROTESTED AGAINST THE DEVELOPMENT OF NUCLEAR WEAPONS.

SOME FEARED THE POSSIBILITY OF NUCLEAR WAR.

OTHERS WERE WORRIED ABOUT THE EFFECTS OF FALLOUT FROM THESE TESTS.

AIRCRAFT WERE SENT UP TO TEST THE LEVEL OF RADIOACTIVITY IN THE ATMOSPHERE THOUSANDS OF KILOMETRES FROM THE SITES OF THE NUCLEAR TEST EXPLOSIONS.

THE RADIOACTIVE DUST WAS THEN ANALYSED BY SCIENTISTS.

The problem of the possible contamination of the atmosphere from radioactivity is important since nuclear power has many peaceful uses such as the production of electricity. At the Dounreay atomic plant in northern Scotland a special steel globe was constructed as protection just in case an accident happened. Workers in atomic plants wear protective clothing almost as if they were spacemen. Exposure to radioactivity carries grave dangers to health and workers in atomic plants are examined by detectors to ensure that they have not been unduly affected by radiation.

After the atomic bombs at Hiroshima and Nagasaki many thousands of people developed radiation sickness – a disease which attacks the blood cells. Since the end of the Second World War there have been one or two peacetime incidents where people have been accidentally exposed to the effects of radiation. One of the most serious was when the Japanese fishing boat *The Lucky Dragon* sailed within 140 kilometres of an American nuclear test explosion and radioactive ash fell on board the ship, later causing the death of one of the crew members.

THINGS TO DO

1. Have there been any nuclear incidents since the case of *The Lucky Dragon* in 1954? What happens when a plane carrying nuclear bombs has an accident? Find out about the cases in Spain and Greenland when accidents of this type actually occurred.

2. If there is a danger that the use of nuclear power can lead to a major accident should the development of this type of power be banned? Or does the pressing world energy crisis mean that all methods of obtaining energy must be developed even if there are some attendant risks?

3. Many nuclear plants are situated on relatively lonely sites at the coast. For the same reason these areas are often jealously guarded nature preserves where rare wildlife species often flourish. Do you think atomic plants such as Dounreay (shown in the photograph) spoil the landscape? How can they affect wildlife? Where would you site atomic plants?

CONSERVATION

Dan Williams, Hilary Johnson, Brian Robertson and Eunice Atkins had decided to form a conservation group at school. Dan's father, a local councillor, had just founded a civic trust group to keep an eye on new developments in the town. Dan and his friends thought they could also do something positive to keep their town a good place to live in.

THE NATIONAL TRUST

THE NATURE CONSERVANCY

THE NOISE ABATEMENT SOCIETY

THE CONSERVATION GROUP MADE A DETAILED STUDY OF THE VARIOUS GROUPS ALREADY WORKING IN THEIR AREA ....

Hilary found out the names and addresses of many other organisations including the Countryside Commission, the Keep Britain Tidy Group, the Royal Society for the Protection of Birds and the Wildlife Youth Service. Dan reported on a meeting he had had with the local National Trust official.

"Apparently they look after over two hundred historic houses and gardens," he said. "They've got stretches of coastline, farms and woods. They preserve things but say if you want to keep them in good order they must be used. They always have projects under way – the restoration of a mansion or the thatching of a farmhouse, for instance."

Brian and Eunice had been to the Nature Conservancy.

"Their main concern is wildlife," said Eunice. "They have nature reserves and they do a lot of research into the ways in which the environment is being threatened. Many important people are involved in their work and if there is any serious threat both the Nature Conservancy and the National Trust can be expected to take some action."

"But we can do it on a local scale," said Brian. "We can become a junior Civic Trust."

"Or Town Conservancy," added Dan.

THINGS TO DO

1. The two photographs on this page were taken within about 50 kilometres of each other in Cumbria. In one view you can see Grasmere lake and in the other the city of Carlisle. In both cases planners and people living in the area are concerned about the problem of conservation. Are the conservation problems of the town the same as those in the countryside? What advice can you offer the people responsible for making decisions about the future of the countryside and the future of our historic towns and cities?

2. Find out more about some of the many organisations which are involved in some way with conservation (for instance the Noise Abatement Society, the National Trust and the Nature Conservancy).

3. Do you think organisations like the National Trust and the Keep Britain Tidy Group are necessary? Why can't matters of town planning, routes of motorways and the preservation of old buildings be left to the local council or national government to do as they think best for the whole community?

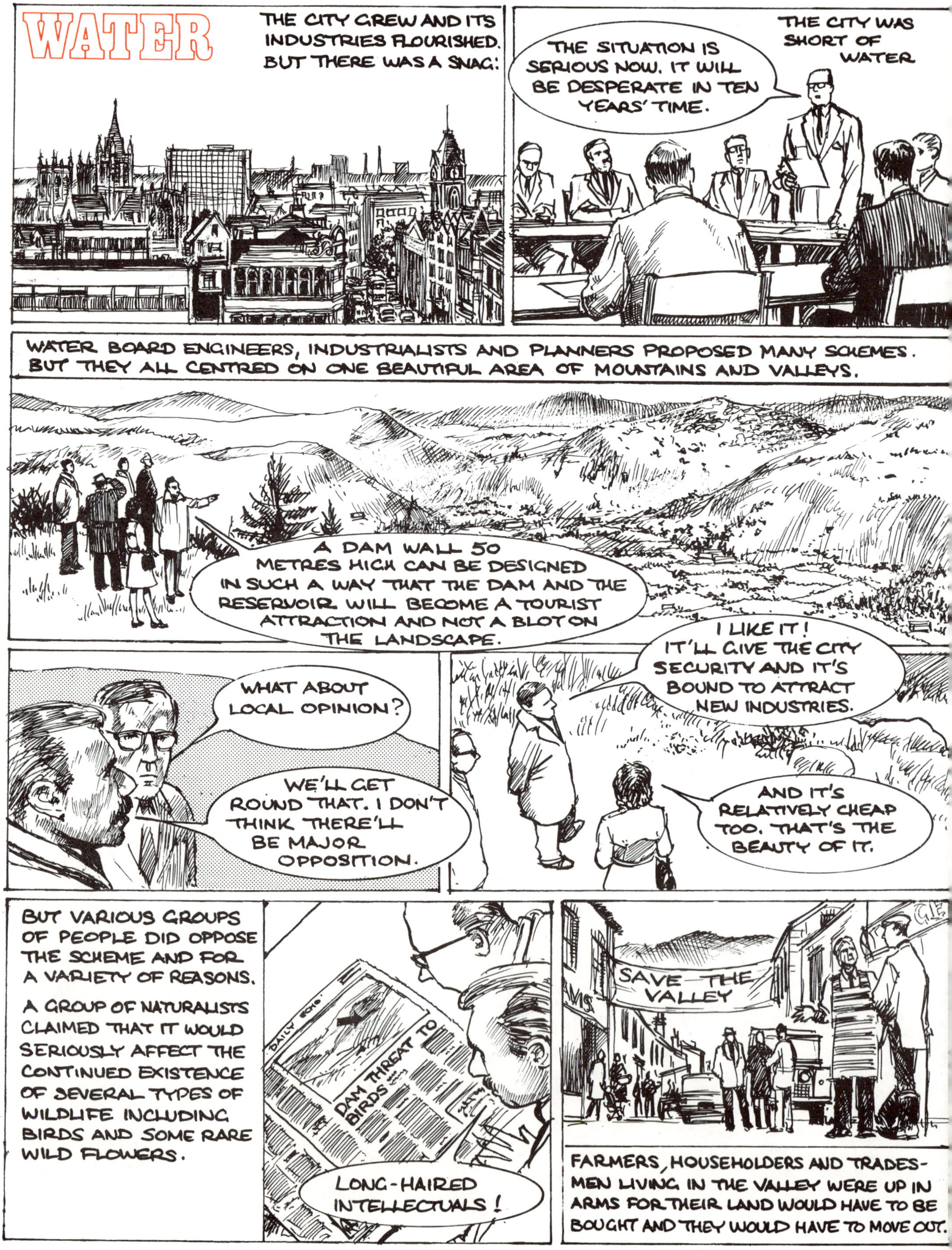

WATER

THE CITY GREW AND ITS INDUSTRIES FLOURISHED. BUT THERE WAS A SNAG:

WATER BOARD ENGINEERS, INDUSTRIALISTS AND PLANNERS PROPOSED MANY SCHEMES. BUT THEY ALL CENTRED ON ONE BEAUTIFUL AREA OF MOUNTAINS AND VALLEYS.

BUT VARIOUS GROUPS OF PEOPLE DID OPPOSE THE SCHEME AND FOR A VARIETY OF REASONS.

A GROUP OF NATURALISTS CLAIMED THAT IT WOULD SERIOUSLY AFFECT THE CONTINUED EXISTENCE OF SEVERAL TYPES OF WILDLIFE INCLUDING BIRDS AND SOME RARE WILD FLOWERS.

FARMERS, HOUSEHOLDERS AND TRADESMEN LIVING IN THE VALLEY WERE UP IN ARMS FOR THEIR LAND WOULD HAVE TO BE BOUGHT AND THEY WOULD HAVE TO MOVE OUT.

The problem faced by the people who lived in the valley was not new, nor was it one encountered only in Britain or opposed by people with a high standard of living. In Zambia tribesmen had to move out of their traditional tribal lands when the Zambezi was dammed at Kariba and a massive lake formed behind the Kariba Dam. The advantages of such schemes are not appreciated by people who have to move out of the land they have known all their lives. They may seem pigheaded and obstinate to the city dwellers who view their opposition as a barrier to progress. The same opposition can be seen when a new motorway is built or an airport constructed. At the Public Enquiry into the reservoir scheme a leader of the local naturalists spoke out.

"We are not cranks. We want to see a prosperous Britain. But we don't want to see a country deprived of all its natural beauty and heritage merely in order to satisfy wants which can be easily met elsewhere. The city has explored other possibilities. Its only reason for choosing this site is that it is cheaper. It is cheap water they want, but what a price they expect us and all who love this area to pay."

THINGS TO DO

1. Do you think the naturalists were "long-haired intellectuals"? How do you balance the need of a city for water against the bad effect that flooding will have on the valley?

2. The old drawing shows Mardale Green, a hamlet which now lies below the surface of the Haweswater reservoir in the Lake District – a major source of water for the city of Manchester. In 1941 the reservoir came into full operation. Since then a dry season such as the summer of 1973 can mean that the tops of some of the submerged buildings in the hamlet are exposed as the water level drops. The photograph shows another valley in the Lake District. Imagine that a dam is to be built which will flood this valley to a depth of 50 metres. How would it alter the area? Is it justifiable to say that because there are many other valleys like this in Britain just one will not be missed? Discuss this topic with your friends

IN 1952 HUGE IRON ORE DEPOSITS WERE ACCIDENTALLY DISCOVERED IN NORTH-WEST AUSTRALIA WHEN THE PLANE CARRYING AN AUSTRALIAN CATTLE RANCHER HAD TO DIVERT COURSE BECAUSE OF CLOUD. THE PLANE FLEW BETWEEN THE SIDES OF A GORGE WHICH APPEARED TO BE MADE OF IRON.

TODAY THE IRON ORE DEPOSITS OF THE HAMERSLEY MOUNTAINS FORM ONE OF THE LARGEST IRON ORE FIELDS IN THE WORLD.

IRON ORE NOWADAYS IS AUSTRALIA'S MOST IMPORTANT MINERAL EXPORT.

OVER 100 YEARS AGO OTHER MINERS COULD BE SEEN IN AUSTRALIA...

THESE WERE THE GOLD MINERS AND MANY THRIVING TOWNS GREW UP IN THE GOLD MINING AREAS.

TODAY MANY OF THESE OLD MINING TOWNS ARE GHOST TOWNS.

ONCE THE GOLD ORE HAD BEEN MINED OUT, THE MINERS LEFT AND MANY BUILDINGS DECAYED AND BECAME OVERGROWN WITH VEGETATION.

One day in the future the iron ore of north-western Australia will also run out, together with the rest of the world's useful minerals and metals. In 1970 it was estimated that all known reserves of oil, copper, lead and zinc would be used up before the year 2,000. Many scientists are very worried about prospects for the future. One expert put it this way:

"If my baby son lives to be 70 he will grow up to live in a world without oil – that is unless huge new reserves are discovered by then. Otherwise he may have to rediscover the bicycle and put the family car in a museum. By the time he is 50 he may have forgotten what a mercury thermometer looked like and may remember the tin can only as a temporary method of storing food used in the twentieth century."

Another scientist added his point of view:

"Perhaps man's ingenuity will help him to discover new materials but there is a limit in the end to what can be used. The problem is this. Should we deliberately save some raw materials now in order to leave something for our children's children and their children's children?"

THINGS TO DO

1. The question posed by the scientist on this page is one of fundamental importance to the future of the world. In the past, as you have seen, when people discovered a raw material they needed – Australian gold, for example – they mined it out and then left the area. They gave no thought to the needs of succeeding generations. In Britain derelict Cornish tin mines, Welsh slag heaps and Derbyshire lead mines tell the same story. At the rate the world's demand for raw materials is developing there will come a time when future generations will be without raw materials unless man can tap the raw materials of the moon, the ocean floor, the planets or the red hot interior of the earth itself. What do you think? Should there be strict control now in order to give future generations raw materials to work with? Discuss this topic with your friends.

2. Write a letter to your great-great-great-great-grandchild to explain why the society you lived in felt it necessary to burn up all the world's oil.

Re~using Rubbish

Alistair went on to explain that several local authorities had pioneered schemes which were capable of making a profit on the rubbish collected by the council's workmen.

"The trouble is that the manufacturers are not always keen to take salvaged rubbish."

"Why ever not?" asked Coral.

"Well," replied Alistair, "it's because the salvaged raw material is not pure. Steel manufacturers say that scrap from old cars contains many impurities which affect the quality of the steel when melted down. When the paper manufacturers use waste paper they have to do something about all the printer's ink which is on the newspapers they are sent as salvage. The world is short of paper so it makes sense to re-use waste paper. But you can see their problem."

"What do they do about it?" asked Jo.

"Some manufacturers have installed large vats where the ink is separated from the waste paper by a chemical process. It's quite remarkable really. They often mix the salvaged pulp with the fresh pulp."

"Can't they do something similar with old cars?" asked Coral. "They are a mess cluttering up the countryside. And just think of all the fuel and raw materials used to make them in the first place. It really is a scandal."

THINGS TO DO

1. In 1974 a protest group dumped great heaps of old newspapers in the forecourt of the headquarters of the Greater London Council as a protest against those local authorities in London which did not collect waste paper separately from other rubbish. Do you think their action was justified, in view of the fact that paper comes from timber and timber is a natural resource which, if properly managed, can continue to be produced indefinitely? In other words, since there ought always to be new timber growing why make a special effort to save paper?

2. The photograph below was taken from a train in South London. When new the vehicles in this pile must have been worth something like £100,000 or so. Do you think special efforts should be made throughout the world to see whether vehicles can be made longer-lasting? What would you do with cars and lorries when they are of no further use? Should they be used as scrap as a matter of course, even if this means poorer steel? Discuss this topic with your friends.

ENERGY CRISIS

"Well it's true, isn't it?" said Mary. "After all, there's only a certain amount of coal and oil left in the earth so what will they use for energy when it's all gone? That's what I'd like to know."

Mrs. Watson chipped in. "Someone was telling me that we waste a lot of fuel. I can't believe that. Everybody I know is so careful. It costs so much."

"I think they probably meant things like cars using a lot of petrol," said Mr. Watson.

"What about all the fuel that is used to heat buildings which are only used for a small part of the day?" asked Mary. "Schools are often only used from 9.0 to 5.0, five days a week. That's just about 40 hours in use a week out of over 160 hours when the central heating is on. The government ought to lean over backwards to do anything to save fuel. For a start they ought to make every local authority in the country build cycleways in towns so that thousands of people can travel to work or school by bike in safety. That'd save fuel, cause less traffic chaos and give everyone healthy exercise as well."

THINGS TO DO

1. The top photograph shows a multi-storey car park in Kendal in Cumbria completed in about 1970. Many buildings in Kendal have lasted two or three hundred years. In view of the energy crisis do you think this building will serve a useful life for a similar period of time? Should we be altering cities and towns to cope with the motor car if it is only going to be a temporary form of transport?

2. What do you think of the argument that we should be building cycleways? Can you think of any argument against this idea? The bottom photograph shows bicycles on a bridge in Holland. Do you see the bicycle as having a good future?

3. Make a list of ways in which fuel is wasted. Plan a campaign to persuade people in your district to save fuel.

NATIONAL PARK

"They can insist on certain building materials being used – like local stone. They usually insist that the building should blend into the landscape, so bungalows are often preferred to houses."

Susan and Tony explored the Park thoroughly and learned about some of the schemes which had been tried out in the Peak National Park. They found out about the Goyt Valley experiment, when cars were not allowed up the valley and people had to use a mini-bus. They met a National Park warden and he told them of the problem they had of trying to cater for the motorist.

"We don't want to stop them coming, but we do want to encourage them to use the Park sensibly. That is why we try to provide car parks and deter motorists from just parking anywhere. We want to see more motorists on foot. They'll see more that way, enjoy it more and at the same time it will stop the roads from becoming cluttered up with vehicles."

"And cut down air pollution as well," added Susan. Later she said to Tony that she didn't understand why special measures were needed in the Park.

"If these measures really improve the National Park why aren't they used everywhere? Why not just say the whole of Britain is a National Park?"

THINGS TO DO

1. The photograph shows a scene in Banff National Park in Canada. Are the National Parks of countries like Canada and the U.S.A. the same as those in Britain?

2. Do you think it is a good idea to say that certain areas of countryside are special areas of great natural beauty and therefore subject to strict control of building and industrial development?

3. How would you answer Susan when she asked why National Parks weren't established everywhere – "why not just say the whole of Britain is a National Park?" Why not?

4. What do you think of the Goyt Valley experiment? Do you think it is a good idea to restrict the motor car in areas of beautiful country?

5. Find out about the National Parks of other countries in Europe and about the smaller areas of land which are sometimes specially preserved – for example, a stretch of coastline.

ENTERPRISE ⵣ NEPTUNE

IN 1965 THE NATIONAL TRUST LAUNCHED A CAMPAIGN TO HELP SAVE THE COASTLINE OF PARTS OF BRITAIN.

THEIR INITIAL TARGET WAS £2 MILLION AND THE SUCCESS OF THE PROJECT WAS SHOWN BY THE FACT THAT BY 1973 THEY HAD ACQUIRED OVER 300 KILOMETRES OF COASTLINE FOR THE NATION.

AN OFFICIAL EXPLAINS :

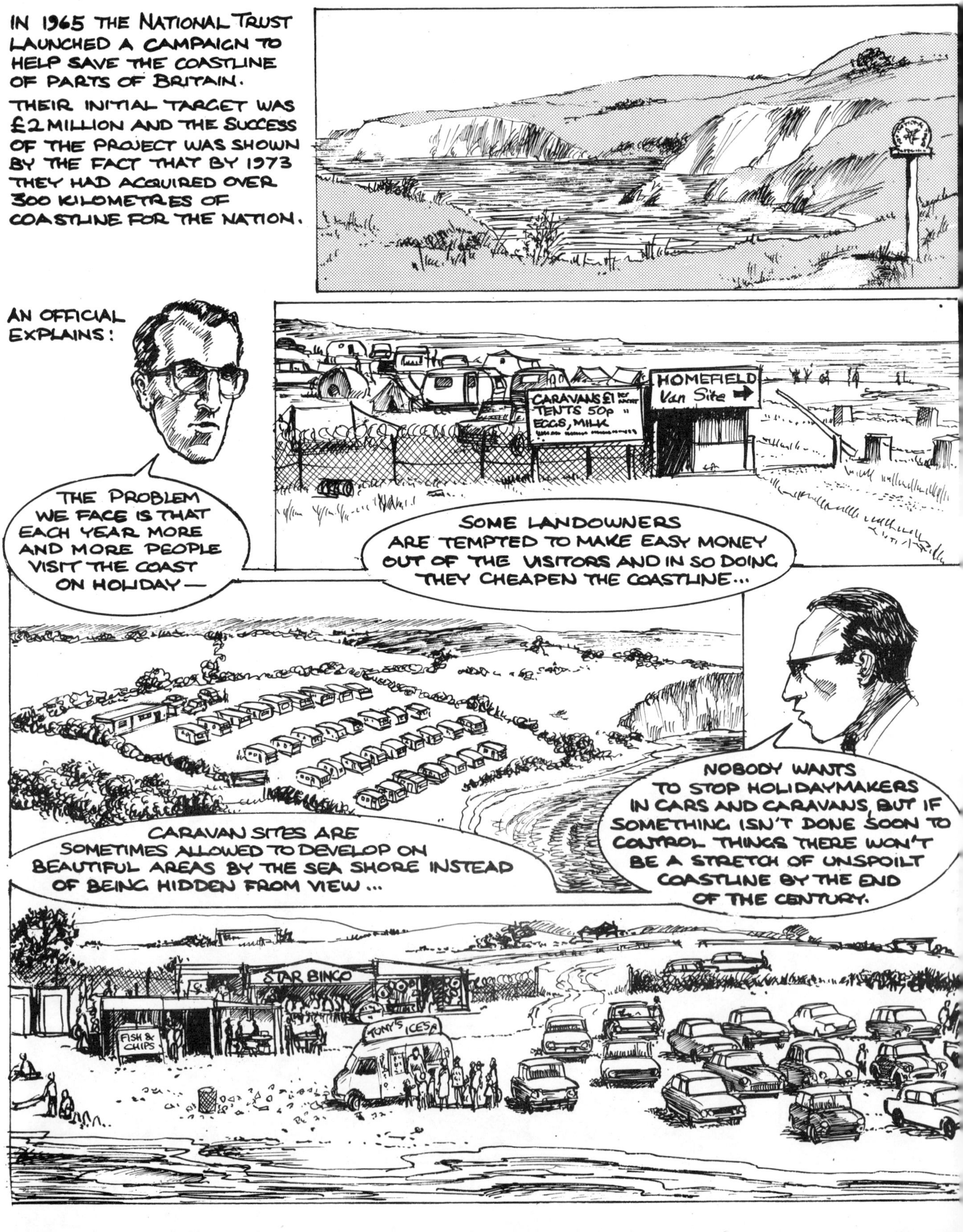

The success of projects like "Enterprise Neptune" will depend largely on the general public. In the end it is in everyone's interests to preserve as much of the coastline as possible as an unspoilt country area by the sea with car parks, caravan sites, cafés, guest houses and funfairs limited to certain sites.

"The public won't stand for it," argued one seaside town councillor. "They have a right to enjoy the coastline and not be hemmed in by restrictions from the do-gooders. It's not everyone who can afford to go abroad for a seaside holiday, so why attempt to restrict people in their own country?"

"Nonsense," said a fellow member of the council. "Have you been to some of the Spanish seaside resorts on the Costa Brava or Costa del Sol? They've allowed buildings to mushroom up all along the coast, just pandering to tourists. It's terrible. If that's how you want our coast to develop I despair."

"Well why not?" said the councillor. "I don't want other people telling me what to do all the time. It's a free country isn't it?"

"Yes," said another member of the council. "But letting people put up expensive caravan sites, car parks or holiday camps hardly makes it a free coastline."

THINGS TO DO

1. Do you agree with the aims of "Enterprise Neptune"? How far do you think the development of buildings, car parks, caravan sites and other amenities should be carefully controlled at the coast?

2. What do you think of the argument that the public "have a right to enjoy the coastline and not be hemmed in by restrictions from the do-gooders"?

3. The photograph shows part of the seafront at Blackpool. Why do you think many seaside resorts have developed in this way? Would you like to see developments of this type banned completely, allowed in moderation, kept as they are or expanded even further?

4. Think about the stretches of coastline you have visited on day visits and on holiday. Were these coastlines spoilt in any way? How would you improve them – both by adding new amenities and by knocking down eyesores?

WILDLIFE CRISIS

BUT IN THE LATE 1950's A PAIR OF OSPREYS RETURNED TO BREED IN SCOTLAND — AT LOCH GARTEN IN INVERNESS.

THE OSPREY IS A BIRD OF PREY FEEDING ON FISH. IT DIVES FROM GREAT HEIGHTS (AS MUCH AS 60 METRES) AND PLUNGES INTO THE SEA, SOMETIMES CATCHING FISH WEIGHING A KILOGRAM OR SO.

INCREDIBLY THE OSPREYS WHO BREED AT LOCH GARTEN HAVE HAD TO BE PROTECTED AGAINST HUMAN ENEMIES.

ON ANOTHER OCCASION A VANDAL ATTEMPTED TO CUT DOWN THE TREE IN WHICH THE BIRDS WERE NESTING.

TODAY BARBED WIRE SURROUNDS THE TREE AND ITS LOWER BRANCHES HAVE BEEN LOPPED OFF TO MAKE IT MORE DIFFICULT TO CLIMB.

OBSERVERS KEEP CONSTANT WATCH TO ENSURE THAT THE EGGS CAN BE HATCHED IN PEACE. IF THEY ARE SUCCESSFUL, MANY MORE OSPREYS WILL BREED IN BRITAIN.

The tragedy of the ospreys is that their existence in Britain may possibly be threatened by man from another direction. Ospreys feed on fish and fish feeding in polluted waters can absorb pesticides such as D.D.T. Already it is thought likely that this may account for the infertility of some of the eggs and the declining numbers of male ospreys.

The Scottish ospreys are visited every year by over 100,000 people. They visit the observation post and can view the nest using a pair of binoculars installed there by the Royal Society for the Protection of Birds. The ospreys are lucky in having been befriended by a large band of enthusiastic ornithologists determined to let them breed in peace. Other wild animals and birds have not always been so lucky. Creatures the world over are threatened with extinction. The list of animals in danger includes cheetahs in Asia, the giant eland in West Africa, the tiger in India and the otter in Britain. Other forms of natural life are also threatened, among them orchids and other flowers. For this reason conservationists advise all who visit the countryside to leave wild flowers in their natural state. As for birds' eggs, it is, of course, against the law to take them or to disturb the nest.

THINGS TO DO

1. The photographs on this page show the capture of a white rhinoceros in Uganda and a picture of a cheetah in Kruger National Park in the Transvaal. Find out how wild animals are protected in countries such as Uganda, Tanzania, Kenya, Rhodesia, Zambia and South Africa. What are the problems in these areas?

2. Why do you think ospreys' nests have had to be defended so vigorously? What possible pleasure or reward could anyone get from stealing their eggs or cutting down trees containing their nests.

3. Look at the following possible causes of the wildlife crisis. Find out as much as you can about them and then say which you think are the most important causes and why:

   (a) farmers' use of pesticides and traps
   (b) hunters hunting wild animals for pleasure or for food
   (c) the cultivation of crops for man on land which used to be the feeding grounds for wild animals (for example the prairie feeding grounds of buffalo in Canada and the U.S.A.)
   (d) killing wild animals for trophies like a tiger skin rug or for a raw material such as ivory tusks.

WILDLIFE versus MAN

"There are other examples you could find to show that wildlife and plants can threaten man."

"Aren't germs and bacteria a form of wildlife as well?" asked Tim.

"Yes," said the teacher. "I suppose we can't really treat any problem on its own. The world is so complex a place that if we tamper with any part of it we can affect other things without realising it."

"Like myxomatosis," argued Jean. "That killed the rabbits but the animals that fed on rabbits had to look for other food. It's like everybody suddenly having a craze to eat sardines. If that happened there wouldn't be any sardines left at all and people who loved sardines would have to look for some other favourite food."

"Are there any other creatures besides locusts which can attack crops?" asked Bob Horton.

"Of course!" said Tim. "Farmers don't put scarecrows up for nothing or use insecticides for that matter.

Locusts are only picked out as something different because they're so terrible, but every farmer has pests. That's why they need pesticides."

"But how do you say whether a creature is a pest or something we ought to preserve?" asked Jean. "Foxes are pests, but if they were nearly extinct they would probably become protected animals."

THINGS TO DO

1. In a famous film the director Alfred Hitchcock once conjured up a world where birds turned against human beings. Other science fiction films and stories have shown plants and other animals taking over control of the globe. What forms of wildlife would you pick out as being the most likely to defeat the human race?

2. How do you say whether a creature is a pest or an animal to be preserved at all costs? Otters feed on fish. Is the keeper of a river which is noted for its fine fish justified, then, in trapping otters? A single tigress was once reputed to have killed over 400 people in India in the early years of this century. Today the tiger is an animal facing extinction. Is this good news or bad news?

3. Myxomatosis was a horrible disease but it had the effect of killing off thousands of rabbits which previously had destroyed farmers' crops. Do you think this was a desirable thing to happen? Discuss this topic with your friends.

Hedges & Fields

TEN YEARS AGO HIS FARM WAS MADE UP OF MANY FIELDS OF DIFFERENT SIZES, EACH BOUNDED BY HEDGES. THESE WERE VERY INCONVENIENT WHEN LARGE MACHINES SUCH AS COMBINE HARVESTERS WERE USED. SMALL FIELDS TOOK ALMOST AS LONG TO HARVEST AS LARGE ONES.

GILES WESTON, LIKE MANY ARABLE FARMERS, DECIDED TO UPROOT MANY OF THE HEDGES IN ORDER TO MAKE A FEW HUGE FIELDS.

IN THIS WAY HE AIMED TO MAKE HIS FARM MORE PROFITABLE WITH BETTER USE OF HIS EXPENSIVE MACHINERY.

When a group of young farmers visited the farm Giles was happy to show them round and he explained why he had decided to clear the hedges.

"I reckoned I could increase my crop yields and I was right," he said. "Tall hedges and clumps of trees shade the crops from the sun and their roots take some of the goodness out of the soil."

"That may be true," said one of the young farmers, "but isn't it a fact that hedges provide shelter from the wind and this shelter can be very useful indeed. What protection will your barley have if there are high winds just before harvest time?" Giles agreed that there were drawbacks.

"But on balance I do grow more crops this way, even taking into account the occasional summer of high wind. And of course I operate my machinery more easily over large fields than over small."

"Yes," persisted the young farmer, "but there is another side to it as well. As a conservationist I feel strongly about hedges. They are a part of our history and not something to be uprooted just to make money. And what about the flowers, insects, animals such as the hedgehog and other creatures which used to live in your hedges. Where have they gone?"

THINGS TO DO

1. Look carefully at the arguments for and against hedges. Try to see the problem first from the point of view of the farmer and then from the standpoint of the naturalist. Finally look at the question through the eyes of the ordinary person who wants food to be as cheap to buy as possible, whilst at the same time wanting to be able to enjoy the lovely British countryside.

2. Find out more about walls in the countryside. When and why were they built?

3. The bottom photograph shows a hedging scene in the countryside of Somerset. Find out how a hedge is planted and how it is repaired.

4. The top photograph shows a typical British farming scene with hedges, trees, fences and smallish fields. Do you agree with the point of view that a hedge is "a part of our history and not something to be uprooted just to make money"?

SIMON HILL AND HIS WIFE JEAN AND SON ANDREW WERE TOURING YORKSHIRE. THEY STOPPED OFF AT PICKERING FOR A CUP OF COFFEE AND GOT TALKING TO ONE OF THE LOCAL PEOPLE ABOUT THE TOURIST ATTRACTIONS OF THE AREA.

Simon and Jean left Pickering and drove along one of the forest drives. The children were very interested in the forest.

"Why have they planted trees anyway?" asked Andrew.

"For timber," said Simon. "We use an enormous amount of wood every year – in the coal mines, for paper, for house building and so on. Much of it comes from abroad. If we can grow timber here it saves having to buy it from other countries. Moreover the trees are ideal crops for land which is stony or has thin soil and can't be used for ordinary farming."

"Are they farmers then?" asked Andrew.

"I suppose you could call them that," said Simon. The Hills had their picnic at one of the picnic sites and then the children asked to go on a forest trail. Simon left the car in a car park, and then they walked along the path stopping from time to time to read the pamphlet which described the things to be seen on the trail.

"They ought to have trails like this in towns," said Jean.

"How do you mean?" asked Simon.

"Well we could have a trail in the park or by the river. If the Forestry Commission can do it I don't see why the same thing can't be done in a town."

THINGS TO DO

1. Find out about Forest Trails and Nature Trails. What is their purpose? Do you think Jean was making a sensible suggestion when she said "they ought to have trails like this in towns"?

2. Some people dislike the sight of large pine forests. Proposals to create large forests in the Lake District have been opposed by people who say that large stands of trees will destroy the beauty of the area. What do you think? Are forests out of keeping with areas of hills and lakes or do they enhance the beauty of these areas? Look at the photographs on pages 35 and 37 showing valleys in the Lake District. Would pine forests add to or detract from the beauty of these valleys?

3. How is a forest "farmed"? How do foresters ensure that the amount of timber grown each year keeps pace with the amount that is cut down?

VANISHING CITY
HAZEL PAGE & AUDREY BROWN WERE ON HOLIDAY AT LIDO DI JESOLO IN NORTHERN ITALY.
AFTER 4 DAYS ON THE BEACH THEY DECIDED TO VISIT NEARBY VENICE
EVERYBODY SAYS ITS THE MOST BEAUTIFUL CITY IN THE WORLD.
AN AMERICAN OVERHEARD THEIR CONVERSATION AND JOINED IN —
WON'T BE FOR LONG.
WHY EVER NOT?
YOU SEE THE LAND IS SINKING WHILST AT THE SAME TIME THE SEA IS RISING.
IF NOTHING'S DONE SOON VENICE WILL JUST VANISH.
HOW?
IS IT SINKING FAST?
ABOUT 5mm A YEAR.
GOODNESS — THAT'S HALF A METRE EVERY 100 YEARS.
MOTOR BOATS DON'T HELP — THEIR WASH IS DISTURBING THE FOUNDATIONS OF THE CITY.

The Delta Scheme, as it is known, came into being soon after the 1953 floods. The first project was completed in October 1958 when a flood barrier was erected across a river near Rotterdam. In 1961 a small sea inlet was dammed off completely and in 1966 another minor dam was completed near Middelharnis. By 1980 it is expected that the entire project will be complete. It will consist of a line of main dams and sea walls forming a long protective barrier against the sea. This will mean that the Dutch will have a much shorter coastline (700 kilometres less) to protect. Behind the main dams there are minor dams controlling the flow of water. As the rivers empty into these reservoirs they will fill up with fresh water. Already Europe's longest bridge has been built as part of the scheme. New industries are being attracted to the area.

Man in this part of the world is winning land from the sea. The sea threatened for years to inundate the Netherlands. The Dutch people retaliated. Their story is not really appropriate to the vanishing world, for they have shown that the opposite can come true.

THINGS TO DO

1. Find out more about the progress of the Delta Scheme in the Netherlands. If there are no books in the school library it is often possible for someone from the school to write officially to the Dutch Embassy and ask for pamphlets which describe this project. Does this scheme point the way for other countries in the world? What parts of Britain could benefit from some form of Delta Scheme?

2. The Dutch have created new land from the sea. The theme of most of the topics in this book is that of the vanishing world. Do you think there are other ways of making more of the opportunities offered by the world for developments which could create new land and resources? Find out more about some of the following projects and say if you think they are worthwhile.

Are they feasible today?
(a) farms on the sea bed
(b) processing sea water for irrigation purposes
(c) reclaiming deserts
(d) altering the climate of the world by using nuclear explosions to melt the icecaps at the poles and then farming huge new areas of land which might then enjoy milder climates than they do at present.

PRESERVING old BUILDINGS

"Yes it is," said Jack. "I bet it's at least a hundred years old. So why not preserve it?"

"Well," said Fiona, "it's not very beautiful is it? I mean to say it's not as impressive as York Minster."

"I dunno," said Jack. "Some people might say it was beautiful. If you sandblasted off that cover of soot it would look much better."

Jack and Fiona carried the argument further when they went into class the following day. The teacher took up the theme and invited the class to form groups to study the buildings in their town in order to identify those which they thought ought to be preserved at any cost (Grade A), those which they thought ought to be preserved if possible (Grade B), those which they thought ought not to be destroyed without good reason (Grade C), others which they thought could be cleared without any fuss (Grade D) and lastly those which they thought ought to be pulled down immediately (Grade E).

"I reckon they'll all be Grade E," laughed Fiona. The class did a good job and the plan they produced with the different grades shaded in was printed in the local newspaper and aroused a lot of local interest.

THINGS TO DO

1. Jack looked at an old chapel and said, "I bet it's at least a hundred years old. So why not preserve it?" What things do you look for in the buildings you think should be preserved at all costs?

2. Carry out a survey of some of the buildings in your town using these groupings:

    (a) buildings to be preserved at all costs
    (b) buildings which ought to be preserved if possible
    (c) buildings which ought not to be destroyed without good reason
    (d) buildings which can be cleared if necessary
    (e) buildings which ought to be pulled down immediately.

3. The photograph shows the old gatehouse at the entrance to South Street in St. Andrews in Scotland. This gateway is about 400 years old and it effectively blocks off the main shopping thoroughfare of South Street. Cars can only go through the central arch by a single lane. Is it worth preserving traffic obstructions like this, even if they are old? Discuss this topic with your friends.

OLD CUSTOMS

CHRISTMAS ISN'T LIKE IT USED TO BE IN MY DAY...
NO, GRANNY — AND A GOOD JOB TOO! THINGS ARE BETTER NOW.
WELL, WE DID MAKE SOMETHING OF IT, NOT JUST SIT WATCHING THE TELLY.
BERNARD JOINED IN THE DISCUSSION
I BET YOU DANCED ROUND THE MAYPOLE ON MAY 1st TOO, EH GRAN?
WELL AND WHAT IF WE DID? IT'S ONE OF OUR OLDEST CUSTOMS. THEY'RE ALL VANISHING, MORE'S THE PITY — LIKE ALL THE OTHER COLOURFUL THINGS IN LIFE.
THAT'S NOT REALLY TRUE, GRAN. LOOK AT ALL THE OLD CUSTOMS WE KEEP ALIVE TODAY ...
... LIKE THE ABBOTS BROMLEY HORN DANCE OR THE UP-HELLY-AA CELEBRATION IN THE SHETLANDS ...
BUT WHAT ABOUT DIALECTS? THEY'RE DISAPPEARING FAST. EVERYBODY TRIES TO TALK POSH THESE DAYS.

"You could be right," agreed Bernard. "You don't hear many really broad dialects these days, that's true."

His cousin Cynthia interrupted the conversation. "Good thing too. This is the twentieth century. I've no time for old traditions myself."

Bernard laughed. "O.K. Cynthia," he said. "If that's your belief why do you observe Christmas then?"

"Well it's a religious ceremony and that's different," she said.

"So are lots of the other ceremonies and customs," said Bernard. "I'm all for the present day and looking to the future but I think it's also good to see some old customs preserved as well. It makes life more interesting."

"Old fashioned if you ask me," retorted Cynthia. "People should spend their time looking to the future, not wasting valuable minutes on things which were important in the past."

"Bet you I can show you that old traditions are still important to you," said Bernard.

"Go on then," said Cynthia.

"Right. What did you do last Guy Fawkes night?"

"O.K.," said Cynthia, "but that's still only one tradition".

"What about hot cross buns at Easter, pancakes on Shrove Tuesday and kissing under the mistletoe?" asked Bernard with a grin.

"Well the first two are bad for my figure and as for the last, it depends who wants to keep up the old traditions. If it's Uncle Arthur the answer is definitely no!"

THINGS TO DO

1. Do you think that there is any danger of the old customs and traditions dying out? Ask your friends and relatives whether they think it is true that the traditions of your home area are fading.

2. Do you think the various regional dialects and accents are dying out? Ask your older friends and relatives whether they think the local dialect and accent is as strong now as it was years ago.

3. The photograph shows an aboriginal encampment in Australia taken several years ago. Throughout the world there are many other relatively primitive communities of people like these aboriginals. Should their old customs and traditions and way of life be preserved, or should they be abandoned in favour of higher living standards and a more "civilised" way of life? Putting it another way — should they be deprived of the good living standards most people enjoy in order that their old traditions can live on? Are we right in assuming that our living standards are desirable for all types of people? Discuss this topic with your friends.

ACKNOWLEDGEMENTS

I should like to thank those friends who have given assistance with this book. In particular grateful acknowledgement is due to Ingram Wilcox for drawing the picture sequences and to the following for their help and for their illustrations:

The Press Association Limited
The High Commissioner for Australia
The High Commissioner for Kenya
The Illustrated London News
Ransomes Sims and Jefferies Limited
William Long
Japan Information Centre
I.C.I. Limited Plastics Division
Tesco Stores Ltd.
Mercedes Benz
United Kingdom Atomic Energy Authority
The High Commissioner for Canada
National Film Board of Canada
The Forestry Commission
The Netherlands Embassy
J. Allan Cash Ltd.
Foto Enit, Roma
Keystone Press Agency Ltd.
South African Railways

ISBN 0 7175 0678 9

First published 1975 by Hulton Educational Publications Ltd., Raans Road, Amersham, Bucks.

Printed in Great Britain by Weatherby Woolnough, Sanders Road, Wellingborough, Northants NN8 4BX.